THE CHANGING FACE OF

BRAZIL

EDWARD PARKER

Author and photographer

© 2001 White-Thomson Publishing Ltd

Produced for Hodder Wayland by
White-Thomson Publishing Ltd
2/3 St Andrew's Place
Lewes BN7 1UP

Editor: Elizabeth Roberts/Aylla Macphail
Designer: Christopher Halls at Mind's Eye Design, Lewes
Consultant: Gareth Jones, Lecturer in Human Geography at the
London School of Economics and Political Science
Proofreader: Alison Cooper

Published in Great Britain in 2001 by Hodder Wayland,
an imprint of Hodder Children's Books
Reprinted in 2002

British Library Cataloguing in Publication Data
Parker, Edward
The Changing Face of Brazil
1. Brazil I. Title II. Brazil
981
ISBN 0 7502 3501 2

Printed and bound in Italy by G. Canale & C.S.p.A. Turin

Hodder Children's Books
A division of Hodder Headline Limited
338 Euston Rd, London NW1 3BH

Acknowledgements
The publishers would like to thank the
following for their contributions to this
book: Nick Hawken – illustrations on
pages 22, 24, 26, 31, 32, 40; Peter Bull –
map on page 5. All photographs are by
Edward Parker except: HWPL/Julia
Waterlow 6 (bottom); HWPL/Tony
Morrison 35 (middle); HWPL/Julia
Waterlow 38; HWPL/Tony Morrison 39
(bottom); HWPL/Julia Waterlow 41 (top).

Contents

1 'City of Success'

The city of Curitiba began its life in the seventeenth century as a gold-mining town. It stands on a high, flat area of land and remained a quiet outpost for many years. Cowboys used to stop and rest there on their way up to São Paulo from the southern state of Rio Grande do Sul.

Curitiba's success story began in the late nineteenth century. Many Europeans emigrated to Curitiba in search of work. They included people from Poland, Germany, Italy and Russia.

Coffee plantations were set up at the beginning of the twentieth century and they provided plenty of work. The modern city of today gradually began to take shape.

By 1950 farms were also flourishing around Curitiba. Soya and beef are still the city's main produce today.

Curitiba is now the capital of the state of Paraná and has a population of over 1.5 million. It is one of Brazil's busiest and fastest-growing cities.

Living standards are high in Curitiba. It is a clean city with good health and education services. There is an efficient public transport system. The crime-rate is low compared to many places in Brazil. The city has plenty of parks, gardens and pedestrian-only streets. Its historic buildings have been well looked after.

These benefits are the result of good planning by local government. Some of the major car manufacturers have decided to open factories in Curitiba because the city is so well managed. They include Volvo, Renault and Chrysler.

▶ *This map shows the main states, cities, and landscape features of Brazil.*

▲ *Public transport in Curitiba is cheap and efficient. This means that fewer people drive cars so the city has less pollution and traffic congestion.*

BRAZIL: KEY FACTS

Area: 8,547,403.5 sq km

Population: 164 million (1999 estimate)

Population density: 19.18 people per sq km

Capital: Brasilia (1.9 million)

Other main cities: São Paulo (10 million), Rio de Janeiro (5.6 million), Salvador (2.3 million), Belo Horizonte (2.1 million), Fortaleza (2.1 million), Curitiba (1.6 million)

Highest mountain: Pico da Neblina (3,014m)

Longest river: River Amazon (6,275 km)

Main language: Portuguese

Major religion: Christianity (Catholicism)

Currency: Real

2 Past Times

In the year 1500 a Portuguese sailor named Pedro Alvares set out on a journey to India. He was caught in a storm and his ship was blown off course. He landed on what he thought was an island, and named it Ilha de Vera Cruz. It was in fact a vast country that later became known as Brazil.

The Portuguese soon discovered that Brazil was rich in gold. Over the next 100 years they forced many of the native people to work as slaves. More slaves were brought from Africa to work in the gold mines. Europeans rushed to Brazil in the hope of striking lucky. Some did become rich, but many others faced poverty and hardship. In 1822 Brazil gained its independence from Portugal. But the huge gap between rich and poor remained.

Early in the twentieth century, there was a growing demand for rubber across the world. Brazil had plentiful supplies of rubber in its Amazon rainforest. Many landowners made vast sums of money out of rubber.

▲ These schoolgirls are standing below a giant clock in Manaus. It was erected to celebrate the 500 years of history since Brazil was first discovered by Europeans.

◄ Ouro Prêto is a mining town in the state of Minas Gerais. Gold was first discovered there in 1698.

But tens of thousands of people who came to the rainforest in search of work died from starvation and disease.

Brazil relied heavily upon imported goods until World War II (1939–45). Supplies from abroad were stopped during the war. New industries had to be developed. Money was put into building new roads and factories. Foreign companies were encouraged to open factories to make cars and other products. The economy began to grow rapidly. But not all Brazilians have benefited from the money that is being generated by new industries. There is still a huge divide between rich and poor throughout the country.

▼ *The whole city of Brasilia was built in 1950 as part of the plan to develop the economy.*

IN THEIR OWN WORDS

'My name is Sabastiao Teciera Mendes and I am a *seringero* (rubber tapper). I live in the Chico Mendes Extractive Reserve near the small town of Xapuri in the Amazon state of Acre. Here I am collecting rubber latex. My ancestors moved to the Amazon during the rubber boom at the end of the nineteenth century. They were hoping for a better life. But my family suffered great hardship for nearly 100 years. The Reserve where I live is named after my cousin, Chico Mendes. He fought for workers' rights. But the lives of *seringeros* in Acre did not get better until after he had died. *Seringeros* were forced to work for no money. Today we have our own co-operative to sell the rubber latex.'

Landscape and Climate

Brazil is a massive country. Its 8,547,403 square km take up almost half of the South American continent. It contains the largest area of tropical rainforest in the world, and has the longest continuous coastline of any country. Brazil is so large that there are still undiscovered mountain ranges and rivers within it.

Brazil is divided into five main regions: the Amazon basin, the River Plate basin, the Guianan Highlands, the Brazil Highlands, also called the Planalto, and the coastal strip.

▼ *The Amazon rainforest covers around 40 per cent of Brazil's landscape.*

Amazon basin

The Amazon basin is an enormous valley in the north-west of the country. It was once part of a large inland sea. Most of the region is less than 250 m high and much is below sea level. Rainforest covers most of the land, and large areas of it are flooded every year.

The River Amazon runs through this basin. Over 1,100 other rivers and streams flow into the Amazon. It carries almost one-fifth of the world's fresh water.

Many people believe that the Amazon basin is the hottest part of Brazil. But this is not true. Its climate is constant, with rain every month and an average temperature of 27 °C all year.

Guianan Highlands

The Guianan Highlands run along the northern edge of Brazil. The area is partly forested and partly arid land. It includes Brazil's tallest mountain, Pico da Neblina (3,014 m). The region has distinct wet and dry seasons.

▲ *The water level in the Varzea area of the Flooded Forest rises and falls by 13 m between the wet and dry seasons.*

IN THEIR OWN WORDS

'My name is Neilson Santos da Souza. I live in San Miguel near Sanatrem on the River Amazon. San Miguel is a village that is on Ituqui Island in the Flooded Forest. The water level in the Flooded Forest changes a great deal between the wet and dry seasons each year. The power of the current has a huge effect on the islands. In ten years, the ones that are here now may have disappeared, or changed shape or moved. Entirely new islands will also have been created.

'When the river is low we can walk between the houses to visit our friends. We also like to go fishing in the lakes. But when the island is flooded, only our houses are above the water. We have to travel everywhere by boat. The floodwater brings mud into our gardens, which makes the ground good for growing *manioc* (cassava).'

◀ *The Pantanal is one of the world's largest wetlands. Pantanal is the Portuguese word for swamp.*

▼ *The Great Escarpment meets the coast at Rio de Janeiro. At this point, mountains stand right on the edge of the sea.*

River Plate basin

The River Plate basin is in southern Brazil and carries on into Paraguay and Argentina. It includes the Pantanal wetland. This area is less heavily forested than the Amazon basin and has more open grassland. There is a big contrast between the seasons here: winter temperatures fall below 0 °C and summer temperatures reach 40 °C.

Coastal strip

The coastal strip runs south for 7,408 km from north of the Equator to the Tropic of Capricorn. It is sandwiched between the Atlantic coast and a mountain range called the Great Escarpment. Mountains stand on the coast from the very south of Brazil all the way up to the state of Bahía. Rio de Janeiro's Sugar Loaf mountain is part of the Great Escarpment.

Brazilian Highlands

The Brazilian Highlands, or Planalto, form an enormous plateau, which has an average height of 500 m. It reaches into almost every one of Brazil's states. It includes several small mountain ranges, the highest of which is near the mining city of Belo Horizonte.

The *cerrado*, which is a lightly-forested savannah, covers most of the region. The north of the Planalto, towards the Amazon basin, is densely forested. In the south, there are grassy prairies. An average of under 1,500 mm of rain falls here every year.

▶ *An electrical storm heads across the* cerrado. *This view is from near the city of Cuiabá in Mato Grosso.*

IN THEIR OWN WORDS

'My name is José Dias de Neto and I live on the Chapado do Guimaraes near the city of Cuiabá in the Centre West. I work as a guardian on a cattle ranch in the *cerrado*. My job is to keep an eye on the cattle. More importantly, I watch out for fires in the dry season. Fires are a natural part of the *cerrado* but many farmers start them deliberately. They think it improves the grass for the cattle. My boss has a more modern approach. He believes that too much fire is bad for the wild fruit trees and animals, as well as for the soil.'

4 Natural Resources

Minerals

Brazil is immensely rich in minerals. There are plentiful supplies of asbestos, bauxite (aluminium ore), copper, chromium, tin, iron, graphite, gold, potassium and zinc.

Eighteen per cent of all the iron ore mined in the world comes from Brazil. The biggest deposits are found in the states of Pará and Minas Gerais. The huge iron ore mine at Grande Carajas in Pará is one of the largest in the world.

Other more rare minerals are also found in Brazil. Ninety per cent of the world's supply of niobium comes from Brazil. Niobium is a mineral that is used in making cars. It is mixed with steel and metal alloys to make them lighter and stronger.

▼ *Gold has been mined at Pocone near the city of Cuiabá since the sixteenth century.*

IN THEIR OWN WORDS

'I am Igor Moustasticoshvily (left) and I am pictured here with my personal trainer in the state of Mato Grosso do Sul. I am the general manager of a mineral exploration company, which is based in Cuiabá in the state of Mato Grosso do Norte. Cuiabá was founded when a huge deposit of gold was discovered in a small stream. That spot is now the city centre. Gold is still mined at Pocone, only 100 km from Cuiabá. The mining methods used there are outdated. More efficient high-tech methods need to be brought in. Then the mining industry here could have a good future.'

Oil

Brazil has major offshore reserves of oil. Its oilfields lie just off the Atlantic coast, near the states of Rio de Janeiro and Espirito Santo in the South East, and the states of Bahía, Ceará, Rio Grande do Norte and Sergipe in the North East. But Brazil only managed to produce 64 per cent of the oil it needed in 1998. The rest had to be imported.

A new oilfield was discovered off the coast of São Paulo in 1999. It is estimated to contain 600–700 million barrels of oil. Even so, Brazil still has to import oil and natural gas in order to meet its requirements.

▼ *The city of Belém, near the mouth of the River Amazon, has a floating petrol station.*

Water

Seventeen per cent of all the fresh water on the planet flows through Brazil. This means that there is huge potential for energy production from water. Hydroelectric power (HEP) already accounted for 43.1 per cent of all the energy produced by Brazil in 1998.

The government plans to build more than fifty new HEP stations. The best places for the stations are often thousands of kilometres away from the cities that need the power. This means that the plans could cause environmental and social problems.

Forests

Brazil's rainforest is the largest in the world. It is valued for more than its timber. Other products include nuts, rubber latex and palm fruits, from which palm oil is extracted. Tens of thousands of people are employed in harvesting and processing work. Rainforest industries generate millions of dollars.

▲ *The HEP station at Itaipu in southern Brazil is the largest in the world. It is down river from the immensely powerful Iguaçu Falls.*

IN THEIR OWN WORDS

'My name is Luis Nelson. I have a farm about 200 km north of Rio de Janeiro. I grow bananas. They are dried and sold in Rio. I also have a few hundred cattle. I have a beautiful piece of Atlantic Forest on my land, where there are humming birds, orchids and other rare species. I made it into a protected reserve, partly because I am very concerned about our water supply.

'The water that flows in the streams and rivers across my land comes from the mountains behind my ranch. Deforestation is causing the area to beome drier. The tourist resort of Buzios, which is only 100 km away, completely ran out of water in 1997. The water shortage happened because of deforestation and a change in the local climate.'

Southern Brazil has softwood forests and plantation forests of araucaria pine and eucalyptus. Timber from these forests is used in Brazil's massive paper and packaging industries.

Timber has also been used to produce energy. However, this is much less common since 1990, because most of the forests near the cities have already disappeared. The trees have been cut down for use as fuel. They were either made into industrial charcoal, or chopped into firewood for local people.

Rainforest and plantation timber could be renewable resources if managed well. But logging companies often clear whole areas of the rainforest to make a lot of money quickly. This type of clearance can destroy whole areas of the forest for ever.

▼ *This man is working at a sawmill in the state of Bahía. The logs are from a eucalyptus plantation.*

Wildlife

Countless rare plant and animal species can be found in the rainforest. Many of our medicines have come from such species. Other forest species probably have medicinal uses we have not yet discovered. There may be vital cures for disease contained in the rainforest. The government is extremely aware of the potential value of these species. It has banned all research by foreign companies so that the profits from any new discoveries are kept within Brazil.

The fish that live in the rivers of the Amazon basin are another valuable resource. The local people catch them to eat. They are also processed for use in a range of fish-meat products, including pet-food.

Natural beauty

Brazil's tropical beaches are well-established tourist spots. Eco-tourism is also popular. Millions of tourists come to the Amazon, where they stay in jungle lodges. Others visit the spectacular Iguaçu Falls and the Pantanal, where the wildlife is easier to see than in the Amazon.

▲ *The catch in this boat includes* tambaqui *and* piripitinga, *which are popular fish for the local people.*

IN THEIR OWN WORDS

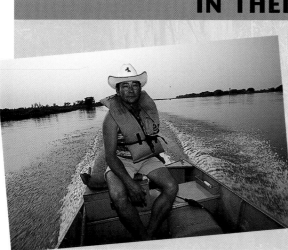

'My name is Rubens Alves. I work as a tourist guide in the Pantanal. Most of the tourists that visit the Pantanal are from the South East. They like to go fishing and I take them by boat to the best fishing spots.

'I have lived here all my life. In the past I worked as a cow-hand on one of the big ranches. But now the ranches need only a few cow-hands.'

Most of Brazil's tourists come from other South American countries. It is a favourite with the Argentinians, who make up almost half of all tourists. They come because their money is often worth a lot more when it is changed into the Brazilian currency. This means that rates of exchange are very important to Brazil's tourist trade.

Tourism in Brazil has quadrupled from 1.1 million visitors in 1990 to 4 million in 2000. More visitors are beginning to come from Europe, North America and Asia. Tourism is growing fast and this growth is expected to continue well into the twenty-first century. It is one of the country's major employers and provided work for 5.8 million people in 1998.

◀ *The resort of Olinda is in the North East. It is particularly popular with African Brazilians. Brazil's busier beach resorts are suffering from pollution.*

5 The Changing Environment

More than 10 per cent of all the world's species live in Brazil. It is home to the jaguar, the giant otter, a quarter of all the world's monkey species and dozens of types of colourful parrots. There are so many species of plants and insects in Brazil that scientists can only guess at the numbers.

All this richness is under threat. The economy and the population of Brazil have grown rapidly since 1970, which has lead to major changes in the environment. Vast areas of the Amazon and other forests have been cut down. Most of the cities now suffer from serious air and water pollution. People are trying to solve the problems in some areas, such as the city of Curitiba and the Amazonian state of Acre. Imaginative plans are being put into practice to reduce deforestation and urban pollution. But many people in other parts of Brazil are not so forward-thinking.

Expansion of agriculture

The *cerrado*, in the Brazilian Highlands, is rapidly being converted into farmland. Much of the area is being used to produce soya beans, which is an important crop for Brazil.

▼ *This Uakari monkey lives in the Flooded Forest. Its future is under threat because of deforestation in the Amazon.*

▲ *This is the natural* cerrado *vegetation, near Cuiabá in Mato Grosso do Norte.*

Selling soya abroad brings money from other countries into Brazil. But this expansion of agriculture is destroying much of the natural landscape. Until recently, the *cerrado* was not thought to have much environmental value. It is now known that the area is home to many rare birds and mammals, such as giant anteaters and maned wolves. Their habitat is under severe threat from agriculture.

The wildlife of the Pantanal is also under threat. At present, intensive agriculture is not possible because large areas are flooded for half the year. However, it is possible to breed cattle here, as they can be moved to higher areas of land during the floods. There were 3 million cattle in the Pantanal in 2000.

The Hidrovia scheme

A plan to improve farming in the Pantanal was put forward in the 1990s. It has become known as Hidrovia. It proposes that some of the rivers are straightened and that areas of land are drained. This would be good for agriculture, but it would destroy the natural habitat of many species of wildlife. Jaguars live here, as well as over 10 million caymans. The plan is not going ahead at the moment because there is no money to pay for it.

Over 270 species of birds exist in the Pantanal. The hyacinth macaw, which is an endangered bird, is found here, in greater numbers than anywhere else in the world. The arrival of millions of birds at the start of the wet season is one of the world's great wildlife spectacles.

▲ *The cayman is a distinct species, related to the alligator. There are many different types of cayman, some of which are threatened with extinction.*

Over-fishing

The Pantanal wetlands provide a habitat for many species of fish. The area is increasingly popular with people who like fishing as a sport. There is growing concern that too many people are coming to fish in the Pantanal and that this is seriously reducing the fish stocks in the area.

IN THEIR OWN WORDS

'My name is Maria Barbosa. Here I am holding a *surubim*, which is a type of catfish found in the Amazon. It may look big, but *surubim* can grow much larger than this one. I run a hotel in the Pantanal. Most of my customers are fishermen from São Paulo. They come here because the fishing is so good. The numbers of fishermen that come here have been increasing every year since 1990. I have noticed that the fish they are catching are becoming smaller. It also takes them longer to catch a fish than before.'

IN THEIR OWN WORDS

'My name is Isabel Ribeiro Coelho and I am 14 years old. I live in Aracampinas, which is a village near the city of Santarem in the Flooded Forest. Everyone from our village is helping to plant trees today. We are planting these fruit trees on the *restinga* (an area of high ground). In a few years they will produce fruit that fish such as the *tambaqui* and *pirapatinga* like to eat.

'Fishing is very important to our village. We hope that planting these trees will mean that we have more fish in the future. I hope that there will be enough fish in the future for us to continue living here.'

Deforestation

Five hundred years ago the Atlantic Forest covered nearly 1.3 million square km of the land close to the coast. In 2002, less than 5 per cent of this remarkable forest remains. The Amazon rainforest has also been devastated. Sixty per cent of the world's rainforests are in Brazil. They cover an area of 4 million square km. The Amazon basin contains the largest remaining rainforest on the planet. Since 1975 the Amazon has experienced massive deforestation. By 1999, forest was being lost at a rate of 17,000 square km each year. This destruction has pushed the Amazon's local people to the edge of extinction. The survival of many species of wildlife is also seriously threatened.

There are a number of reasons for the disappearance of the forest. Trees have been felled for their timber. Areas have been cleared for farming. There are now cattle ranches and massive sugar and coffee plantations in areas that were once forested.

Forest conservation

It is vital for Brazil, and for the rest of the world, that ways are found to reduce deforestation. This is beginning to happen. National parks and reserves have been set up. These give over 42 million hectares of forest legal protection. But many of the areas are so vast that it is almost impossible to police them properly. A more practical solution is necessary.

One answer to the problem has been the setting up of Extractive Reserves. Local people are allowed to collect renewable resources in Extractive Reserves. Many rainforest products, including rubber latex and brazil nuts, can be collected without causing damage. People also gather vines that are then made into handbrushes. The establishment of Extractive Reserves means that forest people can continue to earn money without destroying their environment.

Certified timber is another method of protecting the forest. Only a few trees are felled in each hectare of forest. Chains are used instead of heavy machinery. The impact on the forest is hardly noticeable, even from the air. This method of logging means that forest cover is not affected.

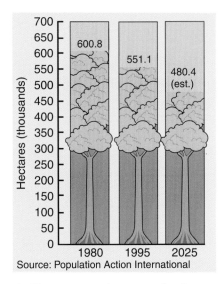

Source: Population Action International

▲ *You can see how much of Brazil's forest has been destroyed in recent years.*

◄ *This man is holding the world's first guitar made from certified timber. The trees have been felled far apart from each other so that the forest is not damaged.*

IN THEIR OWN WORDS

'My name is Paulo Kikuti. I am Chief Forest Officer for Klabin, in the state of Paraná. Klabin is the largest paper and packaging company in Brazil. The company owns large areas of forest at Telemacao Borba. Its plantation forests are a mixture of araucaria pine and eucalyptus, which it harvests every 20 years. Klabin looks after areas of native forest that it has left in between the plantations. The native forests act as natural boundaries and protect the steep-sided waterways. Apart from the forests managed by Klabin, almost all the forests in Paraná have been converted to agricultural land. From the air, the large area of forest owned by Klabin can be seen as an island of trees surrounded by farmland.'

Urban environment

Almost all of Brazil's main cities are experiencing severe pollution. Many people are exposed to serious health risks from both the air and the water. Huge amounts of carbon monoxide and carbon dioxide are produced by the large numbers of cars on the road. Cubitão, which is a centre for the heavy metal industries, is the most polluted city in Brazil. It is closely followed by Rio de Janeiro.

▼ *This smelter in Cubitão is adding to the city's terrible air pollution. The level of pollution here is extremely harmful to human health.*

6

The Changing Population

In 1890 there were 14 million people in Brazil. By 2000 there were 170 million, making it the sixth most populous country in the world. But Brazil has only 19 people for every square km of its land. This means that it has a low population density in comparison to many other countries.

The most populated areas are along the Atlantic coast and in the big cities. People who live in the interior of the country are few and far between, especially in the Centre West states of Mato Grosso do Sul and do Norte, and the Amazon region.

Different people

The Brazilian population includes Amerindians, Portuguese, Africans, Japanese, Lebanese, Germans, Italians and other Europeans. Brazil's first language is Portuguese, but many immigrants still speak their own languages. Spanish is the first language of almost every other South American country.

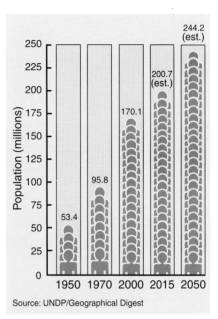

▲ Look at how fast the Brazilian population has been growing.

Africans

Between 1532 and 1850 it is estimated that more than 5 million slaves were brought from Africa. Slavery was finally abolished in 1888. Today, most of the people in the state of Bahía in the North East are black Africans. Some of this region's most popular religions are based on the worship of African gods.

▶ The African culture dominates the North East. This woman from Bahía wears the traditional dress of the region.

IN THEIR OWN WORDS

'My name is Sylvio Bittenberg. I live on a small farm with my wife and family in Pocone. I also run my own small sawmill. My parents emigrated from France to Brazil in the 1930s. They settled in the interior of the state of Santa Catarina. When I was young there was not much work where I lived, apart from farm labour. I decided to move to Mato Grosso 20 years ago. I wanted to try and get some land of my own. Now I have the farm and the sawmill. I have seven people working for me. I am glad that I moved here.'

Amerindians

The Amerindians were the original inhabitants of Brazil. Their population was devastated by the arrival of the Europeans, who brought new diseases with them. In the sixteenth century there were 10 million Amerindians in Brazil. In 2001 there were approximately 200,000.

IN THEIR OWN WORDS

'My name is Bane Kaxinawa and I am 12 years old. I am a Kaxinawa Indian. The Kaxinawa people live in the Amazon rainforest close to the border with Peru. We grow *manioc* in our small gardens and we hunt and fish. We also collect rubber and vines. We make items such as baskets from the vines and sell them to tourists. Sometimes I help in our shop in the town of Rio Branco. I hope I will be able to work there when I am older.'

Immigrants

After slavery was abolished, millions of people came from Europe, the Middle East, China and Japan to work on the large plantations and in the gold mines. Many people in the South still speak German and Italian. São Paulo has the largest Japanese population outside Japan. Both Japanese and Portuguese are spoken in the city.

Urban migration

Brazilian society was mainly rural at the beginning of the twentieth century. Most people worked on farms, or on the coffee and sugar plantations. Others worked in the mines.

The situation has changed drastically over the last century. Large cities have developed and more and more people have moved to them in search of work. By 2001 two-thirds of Brazil's population lived in just nine major cities. The most urbanized regions are the South East and the South.

Problems of overcrowding have arisen because so many people have moved into so few cities. In 1990, the government set up schemes to encourage people to move out of the most crowded areas. Hundreds of thousands of people have since moved from the cities, particularly those in the North East region. Most of them go to Amazonia, or the sparsely populated Centre West region.

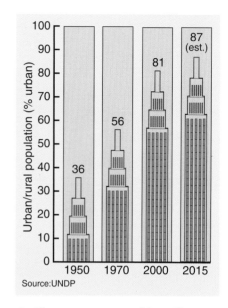

Source: UNDP

▲ *The percentage of Brazilians who live in cities is still going up.*

◄ *This building is in the city of Blumenau. Its design is typically Austrian. The people of Blumenau are white and speak German.*

IN THEIR OWN WORDS

'My name is Senor Da Silva. I am one of the many thousands of people on the move in the North East. My family and I have been travelling around the state of Bahía. We have been looking for a small piece of land on which we can grow food. All the good land is owned by the big farmers. The government has helped us survive by giving us some food. We finally decided to settle on some land that nobody seemed to be using. We cut down the trees and worked hard planting *manioc,* maize and some cocoa. If we can manage to stay on this land for seven years we can become its owners.'

Children and the elderly

The past 40 years have seen family sizes fall sharply across all regions of Brazil. The average Brazilian couple had 6.3 children in 1960. In the year 2000, this average was down to 2.2 children. Meanwhile, the numbers of old people in Brazil are increasing. By 1998 there were 2.2 million more people aged over sixty than there were in 1993. This figure is still rising.

◀ *This retired fisherman is one of the growing number of elderly Brazilians. He spends his days making model boats out of balsa wood.*

7

Changes at Home

Family ties are very strong in Brazil. It is still common to find three generations of a family living in one house. Poorer families often have as many as five or six children. The grandparents help to look after them while their parents are at work. Many children from poor families are sent out to work instead of going to school.

Different lifestyles

There is a lot of money in Brazil, but it is very unevenly distributed. The gap between rich and poor is vast. Some families in Brazil have luxurious homes in the cities and ranches in the countryside. Others lead lives similar to those of people in the poorest developing countries. Millions of people have no permanent homes. It is estimated that 4.4 million Brazilians live in *favelas* (city slums).

▲ *This* favela *is in the city of Manaus. Almost half of Brazil's* favelas *are in the cities of Rio de Janeiro and São Paolo.*

The different lifestyles in Brazil are not only caused by how much money people have. Each region of Brazil has its own distinct way of life.

Life for many people of the Amazon has not changed much in the last hundred years – although they might have satellite television now!

Many of the Europeans who emigrated to Brazil over the last 150 years settled in the South. Today, the region has whole communities that still live according to the traditions of the countries that their families came from.

The people in the South East originate from many different parts of the world and there is an exciting mix of cultures in the region. Most people in the Centre West live in cities. This region is gradually becoming richer. The majority of the population in the North East are trying to make a living from the land. Many people here are extremely poor.

▲ *Rio de Janeiro has beautiful apartments that overlook the beach. There is a huge contrast between these and the city's slum areas.*

IN THEIR OWN WORDS

'My name is Adrian Santo Mendes and I am 13 years old. I live with my family in Cachioera, which is a rubber tapper *colocacao* (settlement) in the Chico Mendes Extractive Reserve. The lives of the rubber tappers have improved a great deal in the last ten years. Most of the houses in Cachioera are bigger and more modern than they used to be.

'We have a satellite dish and a television in the village. We watch football matches on Saturday afternoons. I enjoy living here. I hope I can stay here when I finish school. I want to live and work in the forest like my father.'

Growing middle-class

The people who make up the Brazilian middle-class live in the cities. They work in jobs such as office management or teaching. Most of them have to work long hours because it is so expensive to live in the cities. Their lives are similar to the lives of people in European and US cities. City couples usually have small families of between one and three children.

▲ *Children from wealthy and middle-class families often have access to a computer at home and at school.*

Health

Brazilians have become much healthier since 1950. People have a better diet and access to improved healthcare. Brazilians are living longer because of these improvements. The average Brazilian is now expected to live more than 26 years longer than she or he did in 1950.

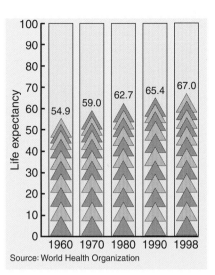

People's health in the different regions of Brazil varies dramatically. The people in the North East die younger than people in other areas. Out of every 1,000 children born in this region, 57.9 will die before they reach the age of one. This is known as the infant mortality rate. The rate in the North East is more than double that of the South, South East and Centre West regions. Much of the population in the North East is also malnourished. In the state of Alagoas 16.3 per cent of the population were suffering from malnutrition in 1998. People in the South and South East live longer and have the best hospitals in the country.

The government aims to provide the same healthcare for everyone. A vaccination programme has been set up, which is succeeding in reducing disease in Brazil. Over 16 million children were vaccinated in 1999. This gave them protection against diseases including measles and poliomyelitis. Standards are improving throughout Brazil, but some states have more money to spend on healthcare than others.

▲ *This chart shows that Brazilians are living longer than in previous years.*

IN THEIR OWN WORDS

'My name is Alexandre Lorenzo. I live in Curitiba with my wife, Rachael, and my 8-year-old daughter, Daniella. We moved here from the small city of Cascavel five years ago. We came because there is more work here and Daniella can go to a better school.

'Today, I work in an hotel and I am also a taxi driver. We have a nice little house in the suburbs. We have decided to have only one child. I will work as hard as I can to give her a good start in life.'

Women in the city

The traditional role for Brazilian women is to bring up the children and do the housework. This has changed in the last fifty years. More people are living in cities, where life is expensive. Women often have to go out to work to help support the family. Over 40 per cent of the workforce are now women. It is quite normal for men to take jobs that mean they are away from home for weeks at a time. Women are left to look after the children as well as carrying on with their own jobs. Sometimes other relatives can help, but often it is the oldest child who has to take care of their brothers and sisters. Divorce and separation are increasingly common.

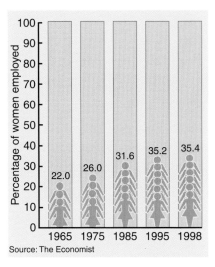

▲ *See how many more women are going out to work in Brazil.*

◀ *This woman is cracking open the shells of brazil nuts. She will not be paid for any nuts that are broken.*

Girls have been receiving higher school grades than boys for many years. But this is not rewarded when they go out to work. A woman is still paid around 25 per cent less than a man for doing the same job.

IN THEIR OWN WORDS

'My name is Aradne Sylvestre and I am 19 years old. I work in a fashion shop in the centre of Cuiabá. My family moved here from Rondonia when I was 5 years old. Cuiabá is still a man's city. There is only one female deputy in the whole state government. Fortunately, things are changing. More women are going into careers such as the law. These types of job have all been done by men in the past. I can even imagine a female state governor here within the next 20 years. As for me, I am like many of the girls here. I like my job. I do want to have a family, but not until I have had a chance to earn some money and enjoy myself.'

More women are going into higher education now. This means that they are able to start careers in areas such as the law, government and medicine. In the past, these jobs would all have been done by men.

◄ *Many villages have women's groups, which look after the rights of the local women. This group is in the Atlantic Forest in the North East.*

◄ *There are primary schools in most of the villages in the Amazon's Flooded Forest.*

Education

Over 95 per cent of children aged 7-14 go to primary school. But many will not go on to secondary school. Children who live in the countryside often have a long journey to secondary school. Some even have to live away from home. Most children in rural areas do not go to secondary school at all. In the North East, 26.6 per cent of the population are illiterate. People in the South East are better educated and 92 per cent of them can read and write.

IN THEIR OWN WORDS

'My name is Maria Marais Cavalho and I live in Manaus, which is the largest city in the Amazon. I am 13 years old and I have six brothers. I attend regular school in the afternoon. I go to a musical instrument school from eight in the morning until lunchtime. I am learning how to make each part of a guitar. Eventually, I will know how to make a whole guitar by myself. When I finish school I want to have my own business. I hope to employ a few other people who can make musical instruments.'

Leisure

Sport, and in particular football, is very popular in Brazil. Brazil has the largest football stadium in the world – the Maracana Stadium in Rio de Janeiro. Football is played throughout the country. The other main sports in Brazil are motor-racing and tennis.

Many people spend their free time on the beach. They play volleyball and show off their bodies. Brazilians like to look good and keeping fit is taken seriously.

▲ A huge crowd has come to watch a game of football on a giant screen.

◀ These men are relaxing with a game of dominoes on the beach near São Paulo.

Carnival

The carnival is held every year in either February or March. A whole week of spectacular partying takes place all over the country.

The street parties in Rio de Janeiro are world famous. Rich and poor people join together in the parades and dancing. The fabulous costumes that people wear have often taken months to make. Many people travel to Brazil from other countries to join in the non-stop partying.

8

Changes at Work

Brazil was a rural society in 1900 and most people were employed in farming or mining. By 2000 most Brazilians were working in a few large cities.

People have begun to move away from some of these cities in the last few years. The number of jobs in São Paulo fell by around 600,000 between 1989 and 1997. Rio de Janeiro also lost 200,000 jobs in the same period.

There are two main reasons for this loss of work. One is that fewer people are needed in the factories because of modern production methods. But another important reason is that many businesses are actually moving out of these cities.

Where people work

In 1989 most new businesses were started in cities in the South East. In 2000 more than half of all the money put into new businesses was spent outside of the traditional business centres. Companies are setting up in new towns and cities in different parts of the country.

▼ *Workers in São Paulo's city centre travelling to work by metro.*

IN THEIR OWN WORDS

'My name is Fabio Martinez and I live in Curitiba. I work for a research company called LACTEC, at the Instituto de Tecnologia para Desenvovimento. High-tech businesses use our equipment to test their products.

'Here I am standing by a special machine that can produce the same electrical power as a bolt of lightning. Brazil often has very powerful thunderstorms. This machine is used to test new bits of electrical equipment to see if they are strong enough to withstand a lightning strike. We also offer other services, including chemical analysis and micro-processor design. Our customers include big companies such as Chrysler and Renault. Many companies set up in Curitiba because there are plenty of skilled workers, and companies like ours offer the services that they need.'

People are finding work in new parts of Brazil. In southern Brazil, the fastest-growing business areas are Minas Gerais and the smaller cities and towns of the states of São Paulo, Santa Catarina, Paraná, and Rio Grande do Sul. Many businesses are also setting up in the state of Ceará in the North East. In the Centre West, most of the new jobs are found in Mato Grosso.

▶ *Cuiabá is the main city in the Centre West to which people are moving. Tourism is growing and there are many food-processing factories here.*

Workers

There were an estimated 51.6 million people employed in Brazil in 1997. But over the past few years the number of jobs has fallen drastically. People have been forced to take whatever work they can find in order to survive. Many workers are not officially employed at all. This means that they do not pay taxes. It also means that they are often paid very low wages and have to work in bad conditions.

This informal work accounts for approximately one quarter of all jobs in Brazil today. Most maids, cleaners and street traders work unofficially. They received an average wage of just US $75 (240 reals) a month in 1997. This is only just enough to survive in the cities.

There were 2.1 million children aged between 10 and 14 years old working in Brazil in 1998. This was a big improvement from 1993, when there were 3.4 million child workers. Slavery still continues in Brazil even though it has been illegal since 1888 and there were more than 600 slaves in 1998.

▲ *These street traders are selling goods in the city of Belém, Amazonia. They make very little money.*

◀ *A boy pans for gold near the mine at Pocone in Mato Grosso do Norte. Many children have to help support their families. They work instead of going to school.*

Agriculture

Many different crops can be grown in Brazil because it has a wide range of climates and soil types. The crops include coffee, cotton, maize, beans, rice, soya, sugar-cane and oranges. What is grown depends on demand from abroad. Brazil is the world's biggest orange producer. Its other main crops are coffee and soya. Livestock is also important. The cattle herd is the second-largest in the world and Brazil is also the third-largest chicken producer.

▼ *These cowboys work on a ranch in the São Paulo state. There were a total of 163,470,000 animals in the Brazilian cattle herd in 1999.*

Agricultural production

Production of soya, sugar-cane, oranges and cereal crops has increased dramatically since 1990. Overall production went up by nearly 10 per cent during 1998–9. But international prices fell drastically in 1999. This meant that Brazil earned less money from agricultural exports, even though it sold more produce.

Cropland has been expanding fast. Between 1980 and 1995, land was being converted to cropland at a rate of 11,000 square km every year. By 1995, crops were being grown on 676,000 square km of Brazil's land. Pasture crops, which produce feed for livestock, covered another 1.86 million square km.

New farming methods are increasing the productivity of the land. These include better soil conservation and improved irrigation of arid land. New technology is being brought in to the North East. Until recently, most farming in this region had been done without machinery. Organic farming methods are being used on some farms.

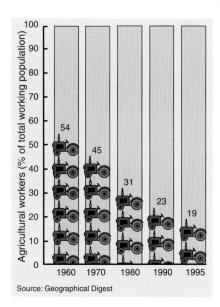

Source: Geographical Digest

▲ *The number of people needed to work on farmland has been reducing for many years.*

◄ *This sugar-cane field was once part of the Atlantic Forest. It is being burned after the harvest to kill off the weeds and stop the trees from regrowing.*

Mining

Brazil is one of the six major mining nations. Around 1,400 companies mine 80 different raw materials, including asbestos, bauxite, copper, iron ore, gold, tin, chromium and graphite. The mining industry grew by 10.8 per cent in 1998 and brought in US $11.1 billion from exports.

▲ *This factory in Minas Gerais is processing aluminium. Aluminium is produced from bauxite, which is a clay-like substance found in the Earth's crust.*

IN THEIR OWN WORDS

'My name is Paolo Guarana and I live and work in Rio de Janeiro. I am an accountant. Much of Brazil's mining and agricultural activities take place a long way from the largest cities. However, large mining companies employ many thousands of people in Rio de Janeiro and São Paolo as clerical, accounting and other service staff.'

Manufacturing industries

Brazil is a highly industrialized country. There were 5.9 million people employed in manufacturing industries in 1997. The factories in Brazil produce cars, chemicals, communications equipment, electrical goods, processed food and drink, plastics and pharmaceuticals.

The pharmaceuticals industry is an area that could bring vast sums of money into Brazil in the future. The plants in Brazil's forests are being studied and new products are being developed from them. A whole new range of health products is already available locally in Brazil.

Car production is another of Brazil's most important industries. The number of cars produced increased from 1.4 million in 1994 to 2 million in 1997. It is predicted that Brazil will be the fifth-largest car producer in the world by 2005, producing 2.6 million cars every year.

▲ *These dried medicinal plants have been collected from the araucaria pine forest in the southern state of Paraná.*

Service industries

Service industries include areas such as banking, computer-programming, restaurants, shops and tourism. They also include transport and rubbish collection. Businesses in this sector do not produce any goods.

IN THEIR OWN WORDS

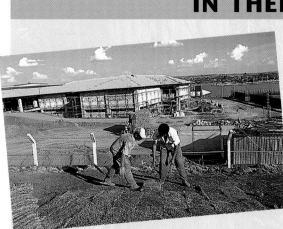

'My name is José da Silva and I live in Goiania with my wife and two children. I have a job in Brasilia laying the grass and the pavements around a new shopping centre. A huge restaurant is being built behind me (right) and my workmate. I work away from my family for two weeks without a break. Then I have two days at home before doing another two weeks' work. I miss my family but I have to earn money where I can.'

A large service sector is a sign that a country is doing well. It means that the people in the country have money to spend. More people work in services than in any other industry in Brazil. Services in Brazil make more money than the total amount made by agriculture and manufacturing.

Telecommunication companies are among the fastest-growing businesses in Brazil. There were fewer than 1 million mobile telephones being used in 1994. By 1999 the figure was approaching 11 million.

Transport companies are very important to Brazil, because it is such a huge country. There are 94,000 buses in Brazil and they carry approximately 50 million passengers. The airlines are another successful service industry. They generated more than US $2 billion in 1998.

▲ *The modern shopping centre in the Amazonian city of Belém is a sign of its increasing wealth.*

◄ *This young taxi driver works in Brasilia. He is one of the many mobile telephone users who are making the Brazilian telecommunications industry so successful.*

9

The Way Ahead

Brazil is often called the 'sleeping giant'. It is a huge country with vast natural resources, but it has not quite 'woken up' to its own potential. Brazil's natural wealth is enormous. It is rich in oil, gold and iron ore and has large areas of productive farmland. It also has a large, energetic and young population. The country seems to have all the ingredients for a bright future. But Brazil has some serious problems it has to address if it is going to be successful in the twenty-first century.

Problems to be overcome

Brazil's economy developed rapidly in the twentieth century and it now has the eighth-biggest economy in the world. Business people are making increasingly large sums of money. But the benefits of these new riches have not reached many parts of the population. The divide between rich and poor in Brazil is one of the largest in the world.

▲ *The future looks bright for this girl. But many other young Brazilians will suffer if the country does not address its problems.*

◄ *The Iguaçu Falls are in southern Brazil, on the border with Argentina and Uruguay. They are a symbol of Brazil's powerful potential.*

Brazil has the largest foreign debt of any country. The government borrowed money from other countries to pay for new development projects. The projects were successful at first, but the huge loan repayments are crippling the country.

Serious environmental problems also need to be resolved this century. Rainforest destruction needs to be stopped and pollution of air and water supplies must be reduced.

Brazil has come a long way in the last century. But it must now resolve some of its most pressing problems. If successful, it could become the most powerful country in the southern hemisphere.

▶ *These logs are from a plantation forest in the southern state of Paraná. Plantations help to reduce demand on natural forests.*

IN THEIR OWN WORDS

'My name is João Augusto Fortes and I work in Rio de Janeiro. My job is to promote rainforest products made from natural rubber. The rubber tapper co-operatives in the Amazon communicate with my company over the Internet. They collect rubber latex and process it into 'vegetable leather'. This is made into items such as bags in Rio de Janeiro.

Our products are sold all over the world using the Internet. Our business is to make money out of natural products without destroying the forest. We think this is the way forward for Brazil.'

Glossary

Cassava A large potato-like root vegetable. It is the staple diet of Amazonian Indians and is eaten by almost all Brazilians.

Cerrado The Brazilian word for lightly-forested savannah.

Co-operative A business that is owned and run by the people who work in it.

Deforestation The clearance of trees, either for timber or so that the land can be used for another purpose.

Economy All the business that goes on in a country.

Eco-tourism Visiting places to experience their natural beauty.

Emigrate Go to live in another country.

Escarpment An inland cliff or steep slope.

Export Sell goods to another country.

Extractive Reserve An area of forest that is protected but that local people can use to collect renewable products such as fruit, nuts and rubber latex.

Hectare There are 100 hectares in 1 square km.

Hydroelectric power Electricity generated by using the power of water.

Illiterate Unable to read and write.

Immigrants People who come to live in a country from abroad.

Import Buy goods from another country.

Independence Freedom to rule oneself.

Irrigation Artificial system of water supply to farmland.

Malnourished Suffering from lack of nutrition due to not enough food or poor diet.

Manioc The Brazilian word for cassava.

Metal alloy A mix of two or more metals.

Migration Moving from one area or country to another.

Pharmaceuticals Drugs.

Plantation A large estate where trees or plants are grown so that the timber or other produce, such as coffee, can be sold.

Plateau An area of high, flat land.

Poliomyelitis A crippling childhood disease.

Populous Containing many people.

Prairie Treeless grassland.

Rainforest Dense tropical forest where there is high rainfall.

Rights Those things due to a person if they are treated fairly.

Rubber latex Milky white sap (liquid) collected by scoring the bark of the rubber tree. It is heated until it forms a solid block.

Rubber tapper A person who collects rubber latex.

Rural Countryside.

Savannah Open grassland in the tropics or sub-tropics with few trees or bushes.

Smelter A factory that extracts metals from metal ores by heating.

Southern hemisphere The half of the world that lies south of the Equator.

Urban Built-up, as in a town or city.

Wetland Land that is permanently soaked with water and often floods.

Further Information

Books
Amazon: The Flooded Forest, Michael Golding, Sterling Publications, 1989
Brazil, Lonely Planet Publications, 1998
Brazil: A study of an economically developing country, Anna Lewington and Edward Parker, Hodder Wayland, 1995
Discovering the Amazon, Readers Digest Association, 1994
The Wayland Atlas of Rainforests, Anna Lewington, Hodder Wayland, 1996

Useful Addresses
Friends of the Earth,
26-28 Underwood Street,
London N1 7JQ
Tel. 020 7490 1555
Website: www.foe.co.uk

The Hispanic and Luso Brazilian Council,
Canning House, 2 Belgrave Square,
London SW1X 8PJ
Tel. 020 7235 2303 ext. 221/2
Website: www.canninghouse.com

Oxfam GB,
274 Banbury Road,
Oxford OX2 7DX
Tel. 01865 312610
Website: www.oxfam.org.uk/coolplanet/

Latin American Bureau,
1 Amwell Street,
London EC1R 1UL
Tel. 020 7278 2829
Website: www.lab.org.uk

Save the Children Fund,
17 Grove Lane,
London W2 1DY
Tel. 020 7703 5400
Website: www.savethechildren.org.uk

Survival International,
11–15 Emerald Street,
London WC1N 3QL
Tel. 020 7242 1441
Website: www.survival.org

World Wide Fund For Nature (WWF),
Panda House, Weyside Park,
Godalming, Surrey GU7 1 XR
Tel. 01483 426444
Website: www.panda.org

WWF in Brazil
Website: www.wwf.org.br

Websites for statistics on Brazil
United Nations Development Programme (UNDP) at www.undp.org

United Nations Children's Fund (UNICEF) at www.unicef.org

Visit learn.co.uk for more resources

Index

Numbers in **bold** are pages where there is a photograph or an illustration